Hide-and-Seek Animals

Kristin Eck

Published in 2004 by The Rosen Publishing Group, Inc.
29 East 21st Street, New York, NY 10010

Copyright © 2004 by The Rosen Publishing Group, Inc.

First Edition
Book Design: Kim Sonsky
Photo Credits: Cover © Milt & Patti Putnam/CORBIS; pp. 3, 5 © Dan Guravich/CORBIS;
pp. 7, 9 © Wolfgang Kaehler/CORBIS; pp. 11, 13 © Hal Horwitz/CORBIS; p. 15 by Maura B. McConnell.

Eck, Kristin
Hide-and-seek animals / Kristin Eck.
p. cm. — (Hide-and-seek books)
Summary: Simple text and photographs demonstrate
animals who use camouflage for protection.
ISBN 1-4042-2702-4 (lib.)
1. Camouflage (Biology)—Juvenile literature
2. Mimicry (Biology)—Juvenile literature   [1. Camouflage
(Biology) 2. Animals] I. Title II. Series
QL767.E34 2004   2003-012821
591.47—dc21
Manufactured in the United States of America

The Rosen Publishing Group's
PowerStart Press™
New York

Where is the frog?

Here is the frog!

Where is the polar bear?

Here is the polar bear!

Where is the seal?

Here is the seal!

Who is hiding in this picture?

Words to Remember

frog

polar bear

puppies

seal